THE LITTLE BOOK OF
PUB ETIQUETTE

First published in Great Britain by Simon & Schuster UK Ltd. 2006
A CBS Company

Simon & Schuster UK Ltd
Africa House, 64-78 Kingsway, London, WC2B 6AH

1 3 5 7 9 10 8 6 4 2

Design: Andy Summers, Planet Creative

Printed and bound in China

ISBN: 0743295331

Dedication:
To Kirsten and Mika

Thanks to:
Kerri, Chelsey, Richard, Pick Me Up, Mum and Dad, Brian,
Fanny and anyone who's ever bought me a drink.

TW

THE LITTLE BOOK OF
PUB ETIQUETTE

An essential guide to British pub culture

POCKET
BOOKS

LONDON • SYDNEY • NEW YORK • TORONTO

Introduction

There is no better microcosm of British society, with all its intricacies and whims, than the boozer. The unspoken rules of pub behaviour are many and varied, from ordering a drink to conversing with one's fellow patrons. This little book will guide you through all of them.

Take a deep breath, raise a glass or two and devote a few hours to one of the most precious places on Earth...

Why we love the pub

The pub is a great place. It's warm, it's convivial, it's friendly – and it serves beer. It's where friendships are made, momentous occasions are celebrated, sporting triumphs are witnessed and sorrows are softened.

Everyone can name their favourite pub, whether it's a heaving city-centre bar or a quiet local in the country. Britain without pubs would be unthinkable – how else would we talk to each other? Let's take a wry look at the unspoken rules of conduct that govern our drinking, as we celebrate the great British pub.

It's a fact

8 million pints of beer are consumed every day in the UK, which equates to 100 litres per head each year.

Buying yourself a drink

Legally speaking, as long as you are over eighteen you can order any drink you want. However, your choice of drink speaks volumes about you. Your income, your status and your background are all on show. Walking into a Salford boozer with a delicate air and requesting 'perhaps just the smallest Campari' might cause a few problems. Always judge the mood, judge the crowd and judge the pub.

Bar staff must be also treated with care. It's no good tutting and waving a twenty about. Remember, in a busy pub you need *them* more than they need *you*. Make eye contact, smile and tell them exactly what you want – they'll love you for it.

Buying Someone else a drink

'Honestly, it's no problem, what can I get you?'
It must never appear to be a problem, even if it
means you'll spend the next week in the
poorhouse. If you really can't afford it, you
shouldn't be in the pub in the first place. We all
secretly do it, but keeping a running tally in
your head of who owes you a drink really isn't
cricket either.

Aggression has no place in the pub and insisting on
another's continued drinking is as rude as an
impolite refusal. Finally, and most importantly,
don't drop it down them when you bring their
drink back from the bar.

Buying a round

Unlike countries where alcohol is more expensive and less crucial to social cohesion, in this country we have an established habit of round-buying. Try this in Iceland or Norway and they'll take a drink, but you'll wait a long time before getting one back.

The best round to buy is not the first, not the last, but somewhere in the middle. Buy the first and you'll wait all evening to make your money back, buy the last and you'll be staggering out of the pub. Buying the 'middle' round stops you looking cheap, but also means people may be halfway through the last drink and not need a top-up.

It's a fact

Cask Marque do all the stuff you hope gets done in every pub, but often doesn't — they check the way that cask ale is being stored, served, and most importantly, the way it smells and tastes. Sort of like a royal taster for beer. They once caught a pub serving beer at the temperature of bathwater (it should be served between 11–13 degrees Celsius).

Accepting a drink

'Can I get you a drink?' may be one of the most welcomed sentences in the British language. 'Yes,' is the answer, of course. However, as in all things, there are rules:

Can I get you a drink?

and one for my friend

1. **Show consideration for the buyer**

   Ordering a bottle of vintage Bollinger will endear you to no one, except the landlord.

2. **Does the offer come with any strings?**

   Gentlemen of a certain age and persuasion still regard the offer of a drink as the first step in a sophisticated dance of seduction. Don't let the temptation of a free port and lemon sentence you to an evening of wandering hands.

3. **Can you buy one back?**

   British pub etiquette regards the acceptance of a free drink without the means to return the favour *within that same evening* as punishable by lifelong banishment to the snook, with no snack privileges.

Borrowing a seat

While a good pub never has enough seats, standing is a bore. To get seated, one must sometimes borrow. This can be a delicate business. The guy sitting on his own may have a date at the bar. If not, does he really want to be reminded of his loneliness by you taking his spare chair? And the big noisy group with one empty seat may have already explained to six other people that they're 'just waiting for a mate'.

Once you've got a seat, the next step is to get it across the pub. Negotiating a route can be tricky. Don't ruin everyone's view of the match by struggling across the big screen with a leather club chair. And never lift it any higher than you need to – an evening's drinking can be ruined by a trip to casualty with a chair leg in the eye.

In summary: **proceed with caution**.

Sharing a table

We all prefer to have a table to ourselves, but sometimes that's just not possible. Occasionally, we have to muck in and share.

The British way is subtle, but final. When absolutely necessary, pairs of drinkers may colonise separate ends of a table with the merest exchange of nods. They then behave as if each of them has a table to themselves. Short questions about the use of the ashtray or location of the toilets are acceptable. Under no circumstances should actual conversation be attempted.

Only when everyone is a bit tipsy should both parties feel free to introduce themselves. They may then buy each other drinks, discover they've both got aunts living in Towcester and make well-intentioned, but utterly superfluous, plans to meet up next weekend and do it all again.

Nursing a drink

There are few better ways to stay warm, dry and minimally lubricated than the pub. However, if funds are short, you're going to have to do some nursing. Half an inch of warm lager allows you to stay as long as you like. Drain it in a moment of thirst-slaking weakness and you're out the door, so choose your one drink carefully.

It's a fact

Over 15 million UK citizens drink in a pub at least once a week.

Look for the best combination of value and size available. Go for two-for-one offers, avoid any kind of spirits unless they come with a bucket of mixers and don't even think about bottled beer.

Taste is the next issue. Under no circumstances buy something you like. This is about endurance, not enjoyment.

Finally, purloin the landlady's paper, settle in an unobtrusive corner and let the time slip gently by. Oh, and stay off the crisps. Salt is no friend of the nurser.

Being drunk

With six pints, two whiskies and a semi-digested packet of pork scratchings washing about in your belly, you're not a pretty sight.

Your enthusiasm for vocal debate hasn't diminished, but your ability to remember what the hell you're supposed to be arguing about went half an hour ago. (As did your mates.) The trick shot you insisted on 'demonstrating' to the bikers at the pool table didn't go down too well. No one seems to like your conga-line idea either.

Later, as you sway gently back and forth at the urinals, a magic little beacon of rationality speaks up. 'You can have another drink. You can have another five, probably. But none of them will beat walking straight out of this place, grabbing a taxi and falling asleep in your clothes. Go. Home. Right. Now.'

Sometimes it's good to listen.

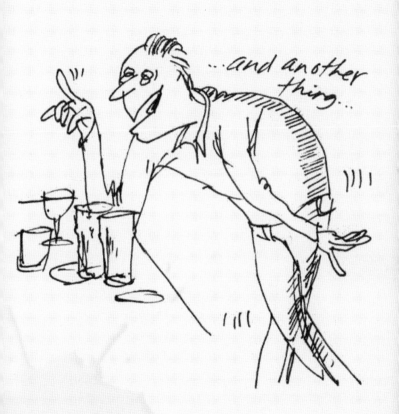

...and another thing...

Dealing with other drunks

Just because someone's had a few too many, it doesn't mean they should be instantly rejected. Some of life's finest friendships can be formed in convivial circumstances. If you decide they're not your cup of tea, there are several options:

1. **Have a quiet word with the landlord**

   He or she often possesses the magical combination of skills necessary to mollify and then quietly eject even the most raucous of boozers.

2. **Pretend to join in**

   By being temporarily louder, ruder and more obnoxious than your foe, you can sometimes stun them into submission. Note: not absolutely guaranteed to work.

3. **The taxi slip**

   Pretend you wish to accompany them to a nightclub for further revelry and hail a cab for the purpose. Make sure they get in first, slip the driver a tenner and watch as they are carried into the night.

...Have you tried reasoning with her?...

Dealing with a drunken friend

If only he wasn't with you. You like the bloke and everything, but he's turned into a right liability tonight. One minute you're enjoying a friendly bit of banter about relationships, the next he's burst into tears at the bar.

Cruel as it may seem, it's your responsibility. You brought him, you take him home. That's what everyone else in the pub is thinking. You may have just bought your second pint of the evening, it may be your last night out for six months, it may even be your birthday. There are no excuses – the drunk is yours.

Just hail a cab, bundle him in and begin plotting your revenge. It's the only way.

Arguing with a partner

Lively social discourse is no bad thing and the pub would be a sorry place without debate, banter and general ribaldry. The precise line-up of the '66 World Cup Team, whether or not traffic wardens have any right to life and the injustice of the local five-a-side ref are all eminently suitable topics for discussion.

Should you and your partner take opposite sides during debates, your differences will doubtless amuse your companions. However, if you decide to have a stand-up row in which your inadequacies as a lover, her shrewish insistence on nightly housework and the general shortcomings of your respective mothers play prominent parts, no one's going to enjoy their evening. Keep it at home, all right?

Pool-table etiquette

The British would prefer pubs with a pool table for every two players. However, economics won't allow it and pubs don't have the space. Getting a game requires interaction with strangers. Thankfully, many techniques have evolved for indicating one's pool needs without having to talk to anyone . These include:

1. **The blackboard**

   Citizens of more gregarious countries may find it hilarious that we need to scribble our names on the wall to indicate whose turn it is to play next, but there you go.

2. **The coin signal**

   No need to ask the players when they're finishing – just place the price of a game in the correct denomination on the edge of the table.

NB. Never accept the offer of a game from shifty characters who approach with a faked air of nonchalance. These people *live* in the pub and take innocents like you for the price of a pint several times a day.

Darts etiquette

Remember the beginning of *An American Werewolf in London*? You don't want that to happen to you. When in an unfamiliar pub and struck by the idea that a game of arrows might be quite pleasant, take some time to make sure that:

a. You're not sitting next to fifteen people in identical t-shirts with darts in their pockets. The board's probably taken.

b. There's not a man the size of a wardrobe by the bar wearing a red satin shirt that reads 'Big Stan – Regional Darts King 1997'.

c. Brian Glover hasn't just told an extended joke about three men in an aeroplane. You may be packed off to the woods and get eaten.

Big games

Thankfully, the vogue for giant games in pubs is on the wane. A few years back you couldn't sip your pint without being interrupted by the clatter of a giant Jenga set tumbling to the floor. Connect 4, Big Chess, Twister – a second childhood was all the rage.

There's nothing wrong with a bit of communal activity in the pub. However, if you've got to spend all night on a giant board game instead of drinking and talking to each other, it's time to look for some new companions.

It's a fact

4 per cent of couples met or had their first date in a pub.

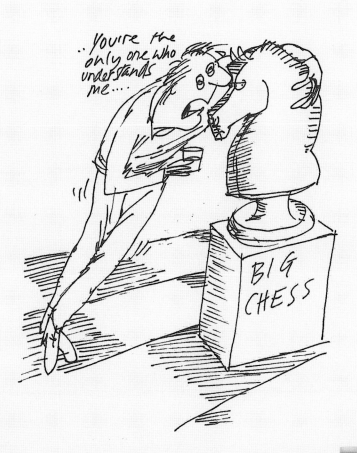

Fruit machines

Everyone knows someone who claims to have met a man who makes his living entirely from playing fruit machines. Such a man may well exist, but that doesn't explain why every other person who plays them is in the pub on their own, piling in the last of their wages and making one pint last for two hours.

The principal function of fruit machines is not to make or take money. Instead, it is to provide single men with some distraction other than staring into the middle distance or pretending to do the crossword while having a drink.

If you're with your mates, don't play it – it's not fair on the lonely. And if you stroll up and bag the jackpot after someone else has pumped money into the machine all night long, do the decent thing and buy them a pint with the winnings.

Using a mobile phone

This very much depends on the location. Londoners barely expect you to stop using the thing, even if you're supposed to be having a drink with them. Venture out into the genteel countryside, however, and you'll likely find polite-but-firm notices requesting you keep your bleepy little friend and his hilarious *A-Team* ringtone switched off. (There's a large plastic jar decorating the bar at the Inn For All Seasons outside Cirencester, filled with the phones of owners who failed to heed the landlord's warning.)

In much the same way that the British don't want to watch you arguing about sex with your spouse, they also don't really want to know where you'll be later, how idiotic your boss was today or any other sordid personal details when they're trying to enjoy a quiet drink. OK?

...Hello Darling — I'm in the @!*!...

Smoking

Gone are the days of having to cut through the smoke to get to the bar. In fact, the new guide to smoking etiquette is simple - just stand outside and look a bit grumpy.

Gambling

Gambling for money in anything other than a casino or bookmakers' is illegal. However, passing the evening with a quiet game of matchstick poker can be very pleasant indeed. Some general advice about pub bets:

Beware of any strangers suggesting games of chance - they are not to be trusted. Stick to wagers on rounds of drinks, domestic tasks or other non-financial rewards, and remember – if you're looking round the table and you can't tell who the sucker is, it's you.

Crisps and nuts

The humble bar snack is taking a bit of a backseat these days, as the rise of Thai menus, gastropubs and other more hearty options provide drinkers with more exotic ways to soak up beer.

However, we British must retain a strong affection for crisps, nuts and other strongly-salted comestibles. How else do you explain the consumption of salted bits of hog fat with hair still in it?

To observe proper snack rules:

a. Buy more than one bag at a time when drinking with friends.

b. Open the pack fully and place it in the middle of the table.

c. Remember, they're not actually a replacement for lunch.

Wine

Not so long ago, drinkers of wine were not welcome in pubs. Landladies would signal their prejudice by storing all their wine in a large, wall-mounted chiller bottle with clearly visible power switches. A small, tepid glass of the battery acid was served to anyone with the temerity to ask for it.

These days, many pubs are more welcoming, more informed and more refined. Today's pub wine-drinker is borne aloft on a giddy sea of Chilean Chardonnay, Australian Shiraz and cheeky little Rieslings. All are lovingly described on large blackboards in language the bar staff have learnt off the telly – hints of butter and toffee, that kind of thing. However, if the bottle the landlady proffers has a comedy drunken fat man on the label, you might be better off with a pint.

Beer

Lager, ale or bitter? Bottle, straight glass or jar? Pint or half? It is, of course, almost impossible to choose, as they are all truly marvellous things. It's hard to go wrong with a glass of ale from a pub with the Cask Marque though – those people care about beer, the Queen cares about hats...

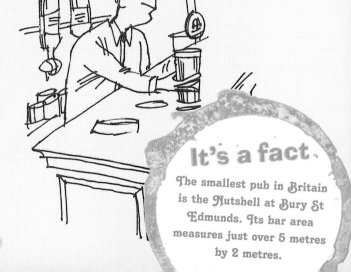

It's a fact

The smallest pub in Britain is the Nutshell at Bury St Edmunds. Its bar area measures just over 5 metres by 2 metres.

48

Tipping

Being generally ashamed of all forms of enjoyment, we British are not renowned tippers. A fancy restaurant might perhaps get 10 per cent, or a chatty cabby a quid. Tipping the bar staff when we're just out for a quiet pint, well, that's taking things a bit too far.

However, a tip can go a long way. Buy the odd drink for a friendly barman every now and again and you'll be amazed. Blackboard says they're out of pies? They might just find one for you. The brewery's just sent us a sample barrel of their new ale – fancy a free pint to see what you think? That git from the estate agent's getting in the way of your pool game? Quietly ushered out into the street.

Good manners may cost nothing, but excellent ones don't cost a lot more. Give it a try.

Last orders

Recent changes to our outmoded licensing laws have allowed pubs to stay open past the magical hour of 11pm, but old habits still die hard. The elaborate rituals surrounding the closing of the pub are hardwired into British psyches.

Goodnight everyone...

At about 10.30 everyone starts to get a bit nervous. The staff pep up and may even begin the evening's cleaning procedures. The drinkers coolly assess the time remaining, the drink remaining and how much they might reasonably consume before being thrust into the street.

PUBS

In every corner of this glorious land all manner of people are daydreaming of their local pub right now. Whether landed gentry or working stiff, we all have a drinking hole somewhere that suits us down to the ground.

Here we explore the many differences of class, status, decor and conversation to be found in the plethora of pubs that lubricate this great and good land.

Sussex country pub

The car park is a mixture of artfully spattered 4x4s (absolutely essential for the dogs and horses, you understand), sleek BMWs, Jaguars and the bedraggled Polo belonging to the barman.

No alcopop two-for-one banners or Sky Sports here. In fact, as the tiny, warped sign consists of nothing more than a flaking Latin motto and a dead bloke in a ruff, you'd be hard-pressed to tell it's a pub. A discreet blackboard announces the game pie, while firmly discouraging work boots and hard hats.

If you're very thirsty, a foaming tankard of ale is acceptable, but get ready for an expensive trawl through the excellent wine list if you're eating. Later in the day, a selection from the broad range of single malts and cognacs is the only way for the chaps, with a nice glass of Alsace Riesling or a G&T for the ladies.

City-centre student pub

What was once a grand Victorian alehouse has since fallen on harder times. If the artisans who built it could see its current façade they would turn in their graves. The pillars have been painted purple and the windows have all been stained green. From a delicate and ornate piece of ironwork hangs the pub sign, which now depicts a cow on roller-skates (wearing sunglasses). Welcome to student drinking.

There are things to recommend it, such as the broad-minded clientele. People who favour shoes with soles as thick as house bricks and have several dozen pipe-cleaners woven into their hair are welcome. The prices are astonishingly cheap too – several lower-priced ales are served by the bucket. And if you run out of cash, they'll let you pay by cheque.

What to wear: anything you like, man, except football shirts and suits.

What to drink: vodka and stimulant liquids by the jug for £4.50.

Free house in a small home-counties town

'Yes, they've just moved in next door. From Welwyn Garden City. Husband's a solicitor. Seem like our sort of people, as long as the kids behave themselves.' The portly gentleman nursing a glass of Chianti by the bar is well dressed. His pink shirt, pressed chinos and expensive loafers speak of success.

The bright, friendly Aussie barman polishes the horse brasses, uncorks the wines and takes bookings for Sunday lunch.

What to wear: something respectable, for God's sake – you're not coming out with us looking like that.

What to drink: a cheeky little Shiraz from the New World should slip down nicely.

Country pub in the north of England

Time was (back in the old days), you could come in here after a hard day at the factory and Doris behind the bar would pull you a pint, put it on the slate and say nowt about it till payday.

These days, things are a bit different, but the old lads still come in for a pint of bitter and a game of dominoes every afternoon. They grumble about the Sky Sports and the way the young lasses get through them alcopops, but they can still tell a tale or two. There's not much happens in the village that doesn't make its way to the pub, and that's just how everyone likes it.

What to wear: nothing that suggests you may be from the city.

What to drink: a nice foaming pint of best.

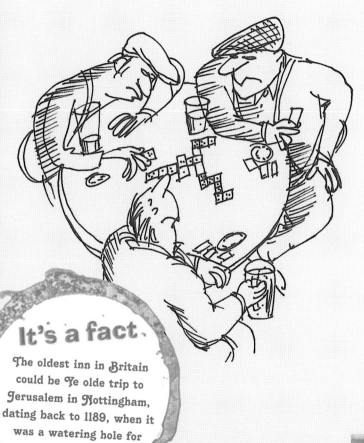

It's a fact

The oldest inn in Britain could be Ye olde trip to Jerusalem in Nottingham, dating back to 1189, when it was a watering hole for crusaders.

Hip West End members' bar

The bouncer is wearing Armani and is extremely polite. Inside the cavernous lobby a discreet sign indicates the bar, which can be reached only by a lift.

You step out into a sleek, dark, fragrant room with the finest view of the city you've ever seen. Beautiful people drink softly-coloured concoctions from expensive, slender glassware and modern jazz tinkles respectfully in the background.

Just to test the barman, you ask for a Gibson. He produces it in a frosted glass without a murmur. You put your card behind the bar, and secretly pray there's enough on it to cover what is undoubtedly going to be an enormous bill. Glancing over at your date with a confident smile, you also hope that they're worth it.

Rugby pub

Monday to Saturday, the pub retains an air of pleasant respectability, but Sunday afternoons are different.

There's an odd device in a glass case by the bar. It's a three-litre plastic bottle with the bottom cut off and a diving snorkel attached to the top. Next to the device is a list of names lovingly painted on a wooden board. It's the 'shotgun' and the names belong to the local rugby team.

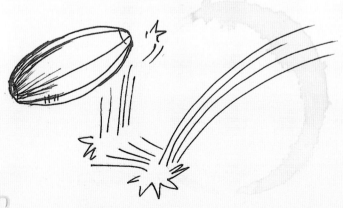

The rugby club test one another's manhood weekly by filling the shotgun with beer, clamping their mouths over the snorkel and then 'shooting' the three or so pints as quickly as possible. Anything under 30 seconds secures hearty backslaps and a reputation for manliness. Anything over, or a failure to complete (a plastic bucket is thoughtfully provided), means weeks of towel-whipping and the worst seat on the team coach. Boys will be boys.

Football pub

In case you were in any doubt regarding their allegiance, the club's emblem is on the wall outside, the big mirror on the wall, the signed team photos behind the bar and inked onto the arm of most of the punters, too. On Saturdays when there's a home fixture, hundreds of fans spill out onto the pavement and victory celebrations can last all weekend.

There's a telly in every corner and a massive screen in the main bar. Radio commentary is piped into the gents. The beer's cheap, the pies are suspect, but there's no better place to show your support. Other than actually going to the match, of course.

What to wear: the right colour shirt. Very important.

What to drink: pints of lager.

Cricket pub

Since Giles' legendary 87-not-out against Badgerton in the 2000 all-village series, he's had a plaque with his name on it behind the bar. Some of the lads give him a bit of gyp about it, but he's still the best player they've got and they're glad he brought the wife and little Gemima down from Fulham and bought the old Post Office.

Thoroughly civilised place, this pub. Cricket prints on the walls, lovely selection of bitters and a very respectable chicken pie, too. Kids can play under the big oak in the back garden and there are summer barbecues. Best of all, the place hasn't seen so much as a raised voice since that coach party from Bolton stopped in a few years back and had one too many port and lemons.

What to wear: sweater, flannels, handmade shoes.

What to drink: a tankard of something nutty to quench the summer thirst.

...Is the chef very temperamental or do they serve the lobster like that?...

Celebrity-chef gastropub

The tables are all blond wood, the walls are painted a discreet rusty orange and the ambiance of relaxed informality is rather pre-empted by the six-month wait for a table.

Big-name chefs all like to show the public just how down-to-earth and hearty they are, and what better way to do it than with a pub? Just stick your name over the door (and the walls, napkins, uniforms and menus), swap the pies and ploughman's lunches for langoustine mousse and foie gras, charge eight times as much as before and everyone's a winner. Except the people who liked it the way it was, of course.

What to wear: your best clobber (there might be people off the telly in there).

What to drink: the best champagne you can afford (don't want celebrities thinking you're a normal person, do you?).

Wacky family-friendly fun pub

Alcohol and childcare, they're a great mix. Someone in a marketing department long ago suddenly realised that people with kids don't go to pubs, because kids aren't allowed in them. The answer? Hundreds of pubs with plastic treehouses in the gardens, novelty fish fingers on the menu and cute little characters on the walls.

All well and good, but the reason that a great many people go to the pub in the first place is precisely because their kids can't follow them. Enjoying a nice, relaxing pint can be tricky when you're simultaneously trying to get glitter out of Suzy's hair, stop Michael from hitting that little dog and wipe drool off the baby.

What to wear: something that wipes down easily.

What to drink: something that looks like Coca-Cola, but packs a suitably anaesthetic wallop.

I knew we shouldn't have brought him...

Theatrical bar

The faces of the greats line the walls – Dench, Gambon, that bloke in *The Good Life*. You know, Margot's husband. Always wore a polo-neck.

Next to all of Britain's great and not-so-great theatres, you will find a bar. Theatrical folk are great lovers of tradition, and the tradition of spending all one's free time wrapped around a hefty glass of malt and telling the one about that time in Tangiers with Roger Moore's valet hasn't shown any signs of dying out.

Wannabe actors and budding hopefuls mix with wizened veterans and dedicated fans, the anecdotes grow ever more poignant and there's the bonus of not actually having to sit through the play.

What to wear: something outrageous, darling.

What to drink: a glass of that cheeky little Riesling might thaw one's bones.

Small rural local in the Cotswolds

When was the last time you saw a pub with a real bar-billiards table in it, let alone one with a queue of expert punters on hand to play? The Lamb, nestling in the gentle folds of the Cotswold hills, is such a place.

Summer sees a ruddy band of locals take to the garden for skittles. The landlady and her husband are plump and jolly and if someone wants to swap a rabbit or a nice bunch of home-grown beetroots for a pint, who are they to complain? The regulars love them too, from the farmhands to the whisky-loving TV writer with his own stool at the bar.

Last Christmas, there was a power-cut, but the pub's got gas, so everyone brought their turkeys and veg over, got the cook to fire up the ovens and had a grand old time of it.

Celebrated Soho dive

A once-lauded actor slumps alarmingly in the corner, a table of film-editors get rowdy across the floor and the American tourists looking for a taste of literary bohemia are edging nervously toward the door, cursing their guidebook.

Tales of legend surround the place. So and so wrote his first novel in the corner by candlelight, this or that actor spent the night in the freezer for a bet and so on. However, it is the truly spectacular rudeness of the landlord that really stands out. Surveying the hordes with utter disdain, he treats all punters with equal and jaw-dropping discourtesy and they love him for it.

What to wear: something scruffy, but clever-looking.

What to drink: the hard stuff and plenty of it.

Bar in a major railway terminus

They were a bit short of original features, but it's not their fault – the place was a WH Smiths until two years ago. So, they've just painted imitation stonework on the walls and some fake windows.

No seats as such, but you can at least rest your pint on a plinth while pondering which of the eight fruit machines to try.

It's a fact.

Years ago, if you fell asleep in a Glasgow pub, the barmaid would remove all your valuables and keep them safely behind the bar until you woke of your own accord.

Bar in a UK airport

As in all things, the British approach the stressful business of leaving the country with a firm resolve and a full glass. No matter how early in the morning, you can always catch a few punters laying into the ale before getting on a plane. Depressing as the sight of 12 ladies wearing identical hen t-shirts, cackling and downing alcopops before breakfast can be, airport bars make excellent venues for people-watching.

It's a fact.

In the last three months of 2005, £3.2 billion was spent on beer in the UK alone.

Airport bar staff are pretty unshockable, too. Think you've seen some things to make your hair curl? Bet you've never had to eject two fat German businessmen at 5.20am for weeing in the complimentary peanuts.

What to wear: an expression of grim determination.

What to drink: something expensive – like you have a choice.

Beach bar in Brighton

As the summer sun sets slowly over the sea on the south coast, the tiny beach bar takes advantage of the warmth to set out dozens of tables and chairs.

Scores of tanned and nubile students are pressed into table service as hundreds of thirsty drinkers settle in. These include tourist families having a rest from the amusements, stag and hen parties on their first pints of the evening, locals colonising the tables and more. All watch the skateboarders, hackey-sack players and other beach types plying their wares.

There's no thirst like a summer thirst and the plastic glasses and rickety furniture don't put anyone off. Once they've got their table, everyone sticks to it, putting all their efforts into snagging the passing waitresses. It's almost enough to make you forget you're in England.

What to wear: sunglasses, slightly inappropriate shorts.

What to drink: something big that lasts – service is hell at this time of year.

Theme bar

Wahey! Nothing says 'fun' more loudly and inappropriately than the theme pub. These places largely exist in the minds of bored punters to fill awkward silences, 'Hey, have you been to that Wild West place down by the curry house? The bar staff all wear cowboy hats and line-dance on the tables.'

If you can't behave yourself in a regular pub, what chance do you have in a place where the jollity is painted on the walls? Irish, Mexican, American, Sports, themes really only get in the way of what pubs are for – drinking.

What to wear: some sort of novelty promotional hat.

What to drink: something brightly-coloured, out of a glass shaped like another, different hat.

Your local

They know your name, they keep your seat, they give you credit and you're still welcome after that embarrassing incident at the pub quiz. There's nowhere on Earth quite like your local. Having somewhere within walking distance that serves a friendly pint and won't give you any bother is one of the most civilised things in the world. It might not be pretty, it might not be exciting, but you wouldn't swap it for anything.

What to wear: tracksuit bottoms you slob around in on Sundays.

What to drink: the usual, of course.

What?

Your mate's local

Everyone knows each other, but they don't know you, so how you'll find your mate's local depends on how popular your mate is. Someone else's local can be a lovely thing – you can make loads of new mates all in one go and feel like you've been there forever. Just watch whose seat you sit in, don't beat too many people at pool and make sure you leave before doing anything embarrassing. *You* might not have to go back there ever again, but your mate does.

The pub at the end of the world

The beer flows in waterfalls by every table and there's always a seat by the fire. All your mates are waiting for you and your money's no good at the bar. Top snack-chefs send continuous bowls of freshly fried snacks over to keep you going, and all your favourite bands are on the jukebox.

People laugh at all your jokes and compliment your clothes. There's no closing time, the beer never causes a hangover and when the quiz starts, you know the answer to every question.

When you finally decide to leave, the only kebab van in the world with a Michelin star is waiting outside. It's followed by a Rolls Royce with a chauffeur to take you home, where you're not too late and everyone's pleased to see you.

We can all dream.

About the author

Tim Wild writes things down and drinks in pubs, with the former sometimes financing the latter. This is his second book.

About the illustrator

Malty, fruity, earthy – Merrily Harpur is an icon of CAMRC, the Campaign for Real Cartoonists.

DISCLAIMER

This book is in **NO WAY** a guide to how much you should drink, or what you should drink when you do. As anyone who's ever had a hangover can readily attest, too much drinking is a very bad idea indeed. Worth bearing in mind.

Lecture over. Thanks.